Practical

ORGANIC GARDENING

David Palliser

The Crowood Press

First published in 1992 by
The Crowood Press Ltd
Ramsbury, Marlborough
Wiltshire SN8 2HR

British Library Cataloguing in Publication Data

A catalogue record for this book is available from the British
Library

ISBN 1 85223 622 1

Acknowledgements

Line-drawings by Claire Upsdale-Jones.
Photographs by Sue Atkinson.

Typeset by Chippendale Type Ltd, Otley, West Yorkshire
Printed and bound in Great Britain by
BPCC Hazell Books, Aylesbury

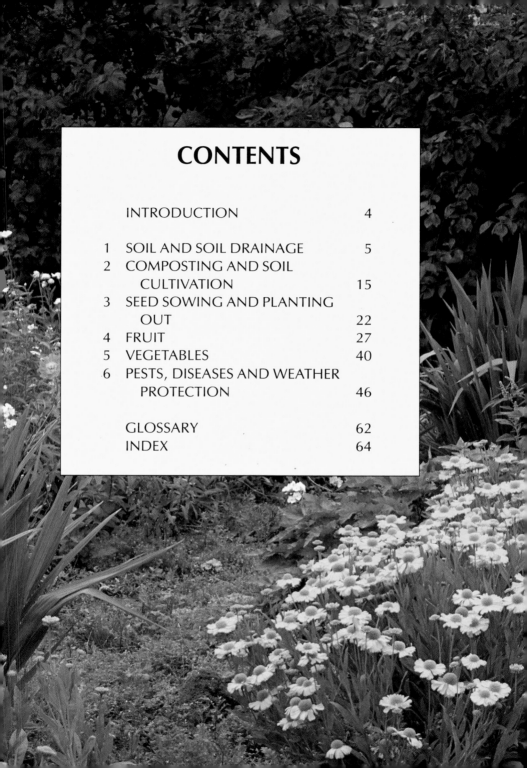

CONTENTS

INTRODUCTION

The object of this book is to give you a general guide to creating a balanced organic garden. It starts with a chapter on soil and gives information on how to get that healthy without the use of artificial chemicals. The first two chapters give a step-by-step guide to improving the soil, for without a soil in good condition you will find it very difficult to grow plants organically.

As well as how to create the right soil, other aspects of organic gardening are covered: flowering times; how to protect plants from adverse weather; immune and disease-resistant plant varieties; and the life cycles of pests — a knowledge of which will help you gain a natural balance in your garden.

This book is only a short guide but by reading it you will realize that creating an organic garden from scratch is not easy, especially when you consider how polluted our planet is. Even when you have your organic garden running properly it may still become polluted. This pollution may take the form of rain contaminated by factory chimneys, fish by-products and seaweeds carrying pollution from the oceans, and on a more local level, certain problems can arise from neighbours who are using non-organic methods.

However, interest in natural organic gardens is increasing and I hope this book will help stimulate you into converting your garden to the organic way. Even if your patch of land is tiny you will have the great satisfaction of knowing that in growing your flowers, fruits and vegetables you are playing a part in preserving the natural balance of the environment.

Planning your garden organically can produce lush plants without any artificial aids.

1 • SOIL AND SOIL DRAINAGE

To plan your organic garden right from the beginning you have to start by getting the soil right. I will therefore start by explaining how soil works in natural conditions and how you can imitate this natural cycle in your garden by making sure the soil is in good condition, drains freely and is renewed using natural composts.

Perfect soil should be free from pests, diseases, some weeds and especially chemical contaminants. It also needs a healthy growth of algae, fungi and bacteria together with soil-working insects and worms, as these help aerate and mix organic substances into the soil. The drainage of the soil is also very important; so take a careful look at the soil in your growing area. Look out for wet areas and the slope of the land, and try to ascertain whether your garden will need a simple soakaway or a complete drainage system. The best time to study the land for water retention is during late autumn, winter and early spring. At the same time you can check for very dry areas and test the pH – acidity or alkilinity – of the soil twice a year in late autumn and early spring, making a note of any differences. If you are not familiar with the soil don't plant the garden straight away, but wait for a year, just monitoring it and keeping it free from weeds. One year of waiting could save several years of trouble and hard work. One of your very first moves is to check the soil texture.

Soil Texture

The ideal soil for growing plants is made up of clay particles less than 0.002mm, silt, sand, and stones and gravel ranging from 2mm downwards. To check the texture of your soil pick up a handful of moist earth and rub it between your fingers. If it breaks into crumbs with a gritty feel it is a sandy soil. This type of soil can be classified as a light soil that is open and allows movement of air and water. If it is very sandy it will need extra feeding and the addition of organic substances. Soil that feels silky and slippery to the touch indicates a high proportion of silt. If it remains as a solid lump with a sticky feel it is a clay soil and will be hard to dig – this type is often referred to as a heavy soil.

To get a soil which is well balanced and which has a good crumb structure you will have to get the balance of clay, silt, sand and humus particles correct as each component is necessary for a good soil.

Clay

Clay soils can become very waterlogged and many plants will die off in such conditions. However, clay is important in forming a tilth (holding the crumbs of particles together) and is essential for base exchange.

Base exchange
When soluble fertilizers are used it is important that the bases they contain are able to exchange with the bases found in the soil particles (hydrogen, calcium, potassium and sodium). This exchange requires the sticky paste that the clay helps to form around the soil particles so that the bases can cling on to the particles.

Silt

Silt is formed from very small particles of silica, but these are only useful in the soil when they are blended with the other constituents and have gone through a further weathering process. Silt can also hinder the movement of air and water through the soil if the content is too high.

Sand

Sand can be either fine or coarse – the ideal is fine sand which can hold the most moisture. Coarse sand will dry out unless a good deal of organic matter is added, although it is important for the movement of air and water through the soil.

Crumb Structure

This is the combination of all the different particles and how they are held together. The crumbs are joined together by the colloidal substances found in clay and humus to give the soil its structure. As the particle sizes of clay, sand, silt and humus are different they will not become compact when they are combined, and so the structure allows the movement of air and water and makes it easy for plant roots to penetrate the soil.

Organic Matter

In natural growing conditions organic matter originates from leaf fall, rotting plants, dead micro-organisms, dead small animal life and the droppings from larger living animals. To consider how this rotting process takes place the carbon and nitrogen cycles need to be examined.

The carbon cycle

Carbon is never destroyed but is recycled and held at different times in the atmosphere as carbon dioxide, in plants or in animal tissue, or stored underground in fossilized plants in the form of either coal, oil or natural gas (*see* below).

Plants absorb carbon dioxide from the air during photosynthesis; some is returned directly to the air through respiration and the rest is turned into organic compounds. In the latter case the carbon will either return to the atmosphere through decay of the plant, be passed on to animals when they eat the plant, or be stored in the earth through the gradual fossilization of the plant over millions of years. The animals return the carbon to the atmosphere again through

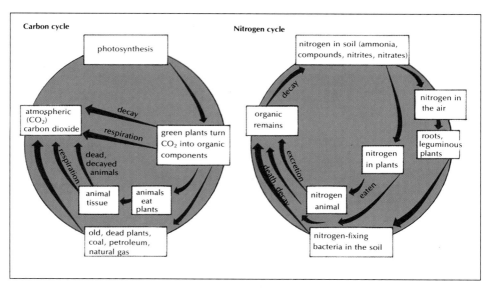

The carbon and nitrogen cycles both play a very important part in organic cultivation and in the welfare of our plants and planet.

decay or through respiration. The carbon stored underground can only be returned to the atmosphere by burning the fossil fuels.

The nitrogen cycle

Nitrogen is an essential element for life and is circulated in the form of ammonia, nitrites and nitrates. Ammonia is formed when plant and animal remains start to break down. Nitrites are then formed when *Nitrosomona* bacteria oxidize the ammonia. Another bacteria (*Nitrobacter*) also has to be present for the third and most important change — the breakdown of the nitrites to nitrates. It is only in the form of nitrates that plants can absorb the nitrogen through their roots. *See* page 6 for the rest of the cycle.

Other factors to take into account when trying to get the best from your garden soil are temperature and the lime content.

Temperature

Organic substances will not break down below a temperature of 40°F (5°C). A soil which takes a long time to warm up will therefore take longer to break down organic matter. The better drained the soil, the quicker it warms up.

Lime Content

Organic substances break down fast in a chalky soil or any soil that has a pH of 6.5 to 7. If you need to add lime it comes in two main forms: either hydrated which is produced from quicklime (as the name suggests this is quick acting and stores for long periods); or as carbonate of lime (either ground chalk or ground limestone). Remember though when adding extra lime to your soil that some plants are lime-haters and need an acid soil to thrive. The classic examples of lime-haters are rhododendrons and most heathers.

pH Level

This is the term used to describe the level of acidity or alkilinity and refers to the hydrogen ion concentration of the soil. It is measured as a scale with the full range from 1 to 14. The low numbers are acidic and the high ones alkaline. A pH of 7 is considered neutral. For the purpose of testing your soil, a simple testing kit is readily available from garden centres. The soil should always be tested before adding lime — any figure above 6.5 indicates that the soil does not need extra lime.

Calcareous Soils

These also have to be considered for they are very common. They are the soils that overlay chalk, limestone and marl. Chalk soils lose organic material quickly because they take less time to oxidize than neutral soils. This means that they may need feeding more often to keep up the levels of trace elements such as iron, boron and manganese. Chalk soil also dries out quickly in hot weather, but conversely, it produces a very sticky combination with clay. Limestone soil is very stony and free draining. This type of soil causes problems in dry weather and needs even more feeding with organic matter than chalk. Marl is a form of limestone which is mixed with either clay or sand. With sand it drains well and is easily worked, but with clay a wet, heavy structure results that is hard work.

Common Plants and Ideal Soil Types

Every area has an overall dominating soil type and by examining some of the common plants that grow there you can ascertain which do well on the different soil types. You will notice that certain species keep cropping up — this indicates that they

Raspberries
Raspberries prefer a deep, cultivated soil enriched with plenty of organic matter. Buy only certified plants to guarantee that they are free from disease. Plant in rows with canes 18in (48cm) apart. The fruiting season is summer/autumn depending on the variety being grown.

Ribes; Rosa; Rosmarinus; Salvia; Santolina; Spiraea; Syringa; Thymus; Viburnum.

Flowering plants
Acanthus; Alchemilla; Allium; Alyssum; Anemone; Armeria; Aster; Astilbe; Aubretia; Begonia; Campanula; Chicorium; Chrysanthemum; Clematis; Convolvulus; Dahlia; Delphinium; Dianthus; Euphorbia; Geranium; Geum; Gypsophila; Helianthus; Hosta; Hypericum; Iris; Kniphofia; Lobelia; Lupinus; Nepeta; Paeonia; Petunia; Phlox; Polygonum; Primula (some varieties); Ranunculus; Rudbeckia; Saxifraga.

Bulbs
Allium; Anemone; Crocus; Cyclamen.

Climbers
Forsythia; Hedera; Passiflora; Wisteria.

Sandy Soils

Trees
Aesculus; Ailanthus altissima; Castanea; Cercis; Ilex; Juniperus; Magnolia; Pinus.

Shrubs
Acer ginnala; Berberis; Cistus; Cotoneaster; Cytisus; Erica; Hibiscus; Hypericum; Lavandula; Lonicera; Rhododendron; Salix caprea; Salix cinerea oleifolia; Salix repens; Tamarix; Ulex; Wisteria.

Flowering plants
Armeria; Dianthus; Gentiana; Lithospermum; Lychnis; Santolina; Sedum.

Bulbs
Lilium; Nomocharis.

Chalky Soils

Trees
Acer; Aesculus; Cercis; Fagus; Fraxinus; Juniperus; Malus; Pinus; Prunus; Sorbus; Tilia; Taxus; Thuja.

are tolerant and so should be considered as good all-round favourites.

Clay Soils

Trees
Acer; Aesculus; Carpinus; Cedrus; Chamaecyparis; Crataegus; Fagus; Fraxinus; Ilex; Laburnum; Malus; Pinus; Prunus; Quercus; Sorbus; Taxus; Thuja; Tilia.

Shrubs
Abelia; Berberis; Buddleia; Buxus; Ceanothus; Chaenomeles; Cornus; Cotoneaster; Cytisus; Forsythia; Fuchsia; Genista; Hamamelis; Helianthemum; Hibiscus; Syriacus; Hypericum; Jasminum; Juniperus; Lavendula; Lonicera; Potentilla; Rhus;

Shrubs
Berberis; *Buddleia*; *Buxus*; *Ceanothus*; *Cistus*; *Cotoneaster*; *Crataegus*; *Cytisus*; *Forsythia*; *Fuchsia*; *Hibiscus*; *Hypericum*; *Ligustrum*; *Lonicera*; *Mahonia*.

Organic Matter

This is one of the most important ingredients of soil composition and one you have to make sure is right before you can say your soil is fully organic. Organic matter is made up of various substances such as plant remains which are broken down into the black particles known as humus. These are smaller than clay particles and unlike the other constituents they cannot be separated from the rest of the soil. Humus forms a substance that sticks to the sand particles and it plays an important part along with clay in forming a crumb structure. It also provides a living area for the micro-organisms in the soil and it has the ability to exchange plant foods, including nitrogen.

To have a truly organic garden it is most important that the organic matter in the soil is recycled to produce a good humus. The humus will then carry out the necessary tasks as described above, removing the need to add chemical fertilizers which may well destroy the soil structure.

Organic matter decomposes in two ways, one of which is anaerobically under waterlogged conditions. The end product of this process is peat. However, the decomposition process which concerns the organic gardener most is the normal aerobic process that involves good drainage, air flow, temperature, pH and the presence of micro-organisms.

Types of Organic Matter

The various types of organic matter can be divided into two groups. The first group contains those types that can be dug into the soil and used in the compost heap. Other forms of organic matter for digging into fresh soil are called green manures and these will be looked at later in this chapter (*see* below).

Farmyard manure
This usually consists of a mixture of cow, horse and pig dung together with clean straw and the straw that was used for bedding – this will contain urine and dung. If you look at the different components of farmyard manure you may find that only parts of the full mix are needed – following is a breakdown of the ingredients.

Cow/pig manure This is a cold and wet manure and ideal on its own if you have very sandy soils. In clay, decomposition may be slow due to the cooler temperature.

Horse manure Produces a good heat when breaking down so is good for the production of warm soils and beds.

Poultry manure A rich manure that needs to be dried and stored before use. If you put it on fresh there is a good chance that it will burn the roots of your plants.

Straw Straw is mainly a conditioner and can be used on its own or as part of the compost heap. Think twice about where you acquire your straw, or for that matter your farmyard manure, because if you buy or obtain it from the average farmer it may contain high inorganic levels from animal feed, weed-killers and fertilizers; and chemical treatments given to the animals themselves, which get into the manure in the form of animal dung.

Mushroom Compost Used after the mushrooms have been grown and picked, this compost can be used as a soil conditioner and on the compost heap. It can be used as a more ecologically sound alternative to peat (*see* key point on page 11) and is also cheaper than peat.

Green manures
This term refers to crops that are grown for

Spread the top dressing by hand, then work into the top layer with a hoe.

the sole purpose of working them back into the soil to help condition it or feed it with nutrients such as nitrogen. Other substances such as seaweed are known as green manures, although in this case it is hardly sown as a crop!

To understand why these green manures are necessary it is a good idea to take a quick look back at nitrogen fixation and the nitrogen cycle (*see* page 6). Nitrogen-fixing bacteria (those that convert ammonia into nitrites and nitrates) not only live in the soil but are also found in nodules on the roots of leguminous plants.

During the lives of these plants a symbiotic relationship exists between the bacteria and the plants – the plant provides sugar and organic carbon for the bacteria and in turn the bacteria provide nitrogen for the plant. Digging these plants into

the soil therefore increases its nitrogen content.

Cultivation of these green manure crops is not very practical for the average gardener, but with the increasing availability of ready-prepared organic green manures life is becoming easier. A quick run-down of what each one does best is useful: broad bean is a classic nitrogen fixer when worked back into the soil; peas act in a similar way; clover again is a rich nitrogen fixer and should be dug in two to three weeks before planting your crops.

During rest periods for the soil the following green manures can be grown: alfalfa; buckwheat; and mustard. Other forms of organic matter traditionally available are: spent hops – ideal as a soil conditioner when applied at 11–18oz per sq yd (300–500g per sq m); cattle cake – the sweepings from this product can be applied to an area for added nitrogen at the rate of 10oz per sq yd (270g per sq m); feathers – these also contain nitrogen which can be utilized when worked into the soil at 10oz per sq yd (270g per sq m); and shoddy which is the wool, cloth and silk left-overs of textile industries – but watch out for contamination with inorganic chemicals and dyes.

Concentrated organic manures
In this section on organic matter we have looked at manures that improve the physical condition of the soil and add body to it. There is another group of products that offer the soil and plants more food – they are concentrated organic manures and ,they have to be changed into nitrates by the soil bacteria before the plants can utilize them.

There are two forms, quick release and slow release. The slow-release type takes several months to release its nutrients, but with the quick form you should make sure your plants are already planted before applying.

Quick-acting concentrates Dried blood contains nitrogen and phosphoric acid, and the rates at which it should be applied are usually given by the manufacturer. Fish guano is made from fish after the oil has been removed and includes up to 9 per cent of nitrogen and phosphoric acid. This concentrate acts quickly and needs to ̇ be applied in advance or root systems may be burnt. Wood ash contains mineral salts, but make sure you use ash from only clean, non-diseased and uncontaminated wood. Wood ash will supply up to 5 per cent potash and other materials. Apply this concentrate at the rate of 4.5–9 oz per sq yd (130–250g per sq m).

Slow-release concentrates Hoof and horn should be purchased in the fine powder form used for potting – do not purchase the gritty powder as it takes too long to

---

To peat or not to peat
One of the best organic mulches and additives over the years has been peat, but such has been its use by commercial garden product manufacturers that the peat bogs in Western Europe are rapidly disappearing. Because of the time these peat bogs take to form, their conservation is now very important. A true organic gardener who cares for the natural environment should refrain from using any products with a peat content. There are a number of alternatives currently available for mulching, the most interesting being the waste fibre from cocoa shells and coconuts. In Africa and the Far East there are piles of these waste products that have been discarded during manufacturing processes. They make excellent garden mulches and contain natural gums that can bind together to form a moisture-retaining mat. They also contain small amounts of nitrogen, potash, phosphates and magnesium which leach into the soil as the mulch breaks down – thus improving the humus content of the soil. These products and some other alternatives are becoming more commercially available, so keep your eye out for them and try them in your garden.

---

break down. This concentrate supplies 7–14 per cent of nitrogen and should be dug into the soil before planting. Steamed bonemeal is made from boiled bones ground to a powder and contains 20–30 per cent phosphoric acid.

Soil Chemicals

Major elements are needed in large amounts in the soil. Major elements act upon the main growing sections of the plant while trace elements work in smaller amounts acting as catalysts and speeding up major element reactions.

Major elements
The first three to mention are carbon, hydrogen and oxygen, and these are found in

air and water. All the other major elements are present in the soil or can be added by feeding it with organic matter. Each one is described below briefly along with the symptoms of deficiency and the causes for this deficiency.

Nitrogen Plants use this element for most major growth processes and it also helps with the formation of chlorophyll. A nitrogen-deficient plant will be stunted and have an off-yellow/green colour. Deficiency is caused by a lack of organic matter, a cold, waterlogged or poorly drained soil, a low pH level or a low bacterial action.

Phosphorus This is important to the formation of plant cells. When a plant is deficient of phosphorous there is poor root growth and the plant colour becomes dull. Phosphorus deficiency occurs as a result of a lack of organic matter, a pH which is too low or waterlogged and poorly drained soils.

Potassium This chemical builds resistance to disease and regulates the sap flow. Deficiency causes leaves to turn blue/green and brown marks appear on the tips of shoots. Deficiency usually occurs in free-draining sandy and chalk soils.

Calcium This is important in above-ground growth and for strengthening cells in the root tips. A lack of calcium gives poor root growth and poor leaf tips, and a deficiency is caused by acidic soils with low pH.

Magnesium This helps to form chlorophyll and assists in seed formation along with phosphorous. When deficient, the old leaves of the plant turn a yellowy-green colour. Deficiency occurs in sandy soils which lack organic matter.

Trace elements

Manganese This is required for the formation of chlorophyll. Deficiency results in yellow leaves and occurs on over-limed or chalky soil.

Iron This also helps in the formation of chlorophyll. Deficiency results in yellow plants and generally occurs on chalky or over-limed soils.

Boron This element helps with the absorption of major elements. A deficiency results in the disease called canker and occurs when the soil is too open and sandy.

Molybdnemum This is important for nitrogen fixation and a deficiency results in whiptail disease. Deficiency occurs when the soil is too acid.

Soil Drainage

Now that you have determined the soil type and a pH level your next task is to look at drainage problems on your land. If the soil is too free draining more organic matter must be applied, but the real problems start with poorly drained soils. The only way to improve this is by constructing some form of drainage system.

Drainage Systems

The two main types of drainage system are a simple soakaway or a more elaborate system of pipes. The choice depends on how the land drains.

Soakaways

The most simple form of drainage is the soakaway. It is useful if you find that the levels in your garden all run the same way so water collects in one area. The soakaway should be constructed in the area where the water stays longest, or at the lowest part of the garden.

Mark a 1–2sq yd (1–2sq m) area then dig down 3–6ft (1–2m) or to the water table if it is nearer the surface. If you are going to dig down 6ft (2m) shore up the walls as you go to stop them from collapsing.

Once the soakaway has been dug to the required level place bricks up all four sides, and fill in the hole with broken bricks and

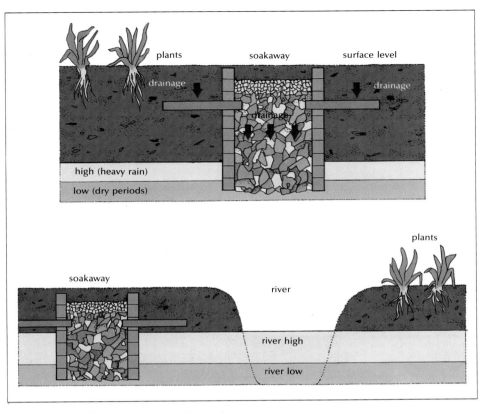

The water table will govern the depth of the soakaway.

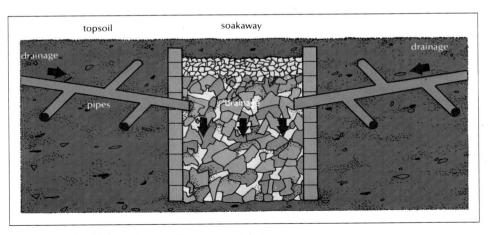

Hardcore used to fill the soakaway will ensure good drainage.

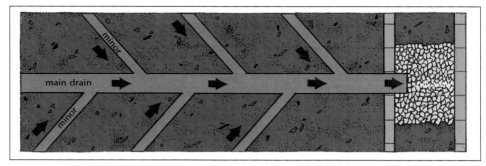

The minor drains take the water to the main drain which leads to the soakaway.

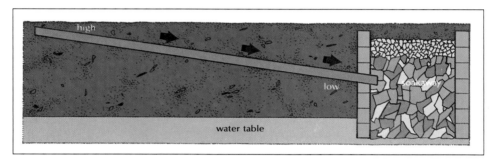

All pipework should slope towards the soakaway.

stones. On top of the rubble place coarse pea shingle and fill the remainder of the hole with top soil. On the top either lay turf, sow grass seed or cover it with a lid.

Pipe systems

If you find the water lies on the surface in several places you will need a drainage system of interconnecting pipes. In this case you will still need to dig a soakaway at an appropriate point for the pipes to lead into. When bricking up the walls of the soakaway leave holes in the walls to take the pipes.

To lay the drainage pipes first mark out the area that is to be dug. If the soakaway is at one end of the garden then one main drain with several minor drains should do.

If the soakaway has to be in the centre of the garden then two to four main drains with minor drains branching off may be necessary.

Dig the trenches 1.5–3ft (0.5m–1m) deep for main drains and slightly less for minor drains. The exact depth measurement depends on the type of soil: clay soil should have pipes closer to the surface than sandier types. Allow a slight fall towards the soakaway for the minor and main drains and lay at an angle of 3ft to every 60yd (1m to every 60m) of fall. Fill the trench with coarse pea shingle and finish off with top soil. Do not forget to make a note of where the drains are so that you can find them if repairs are necessary and can avoid breaking them when you are digging.

2 • COMPOSTING AND SOIL CULTIVATION

The next step in converting your garden into a truly organic state is to consider the compost heap and your store of organic matter.

Storing Organic Matter

Storing organic matter is not the same as keeping a normal compost heap. The new raw materials (cow manure, horse manure, pig manure and straw) must be stored before use. If used fresh these materials would burn the root systems of plants – the straw is also easier to apply and mix when it has partially decomposed. The storage period lasts for between six and twelve months.

Storing Manure

Manures need storing in a bay, so pick a suitable, clean area in your garden, lay a concrete base, and then build a three-sided wood or brick construction without gaps. A removable wooden, slanting roof or black plastic can be used to top off the bay which

Collecting the waste products for creating the compost for next year.

will keep out the rain – rain falling on the manure would result in a loss of nitrogen. The manure should not be stored in heaps and air should not be allowed to pass through it as this causes a loss of materials. Tread down the top of the manure after stacking as this will help pack it.

It is worth noting that some types of manure contain more moisture than others

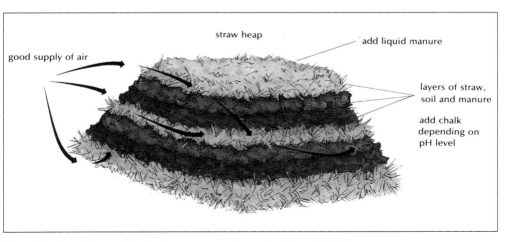

straw heap

add liquid manure

good supply of air

layers of straw, soil and manure

add chalk depending on pH level

A combination of straw and liquid horse manure makes an ideal organic fertilizer.

A simple store for organic waste; cover with plastic to protect from excessive rain.

Add nettles to the waste products as they act as an accelerator for the compost heap.

and so they warm up at different rates. Poultry manure, for instance, is very rich and hot, so when you store this substance your heap should contain alternate layers of manure and soil.

Storing Straw

Straw should be partially decomposed before you mix it with soil so, like manure, it needs storing. However, it needs a good supply of air and moisture, although it should not be too wet. The best straw to use is either that which has been soaked with water or that which has been used as animal bedding and covered with urine. You should also apply a form of liquid manure to the straw to help speed up the rotting process. Soil and manure should be added to each layer of the heap to encourage bacteria, and chalk added to keep the pH at about neutral.

Grass Cuttings

Grass cuttings can be composted with other waste products or stored in the same way as straw.

The Compost Heap

This is your major source of organic material, so a constant supply of raw organic matter is necessary. As well as obtaining supplies of manure and straw you should also take the time to store and use kitchen waste such as off-cuts from green vegetables, potato peelings, onion skins, leftover fish and so on.

Building a Compost Heap

To create your compost heap you will need

to pick a clean part of the garden. It should be away from the house as it will give off odour; also try to screen it from view for aesthetic reasons. A small compost unit can be purchased from garden centres, or you can build your own if you have a large garden. There are two main composting systems: those in layers or those which use a series of bays.

Composting in layers

To follow this method build the layers 1ft (30cm) thick over an area of 10–20sq ft (1–2sq m). The first layer should contain straw, soil, household waste and some form of manure. Tread this layer down and water, but do not waterlog. Spread a thin layer of soil over the top next and then another layer of mixed organic material. Continue in this sequence, building the

heap and making sure that the sides are sloping, until you get to a height of about 5ft (1.5m). If the soil you used in the heap had a pH of less than 7 then lime should be added to the heap.

The heap should be watered every two weeks and turned every five to six weeks – this is hard work but is important for speeding up the rotting process. If you think this method is too much work use the bay system instead.

Composting in bays

Mark out a clean area and then, if desired although this is not essential, lay a concrete base. Build three wooden bays with gaps between the planks. The first is used for storing and collecting raw material, the second for the breakdown stage and the third for material ready for use. Place

A compost bay is easy to make from old wooden boards.

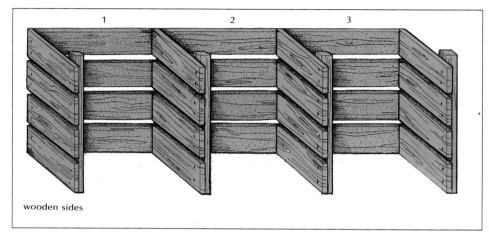

A three-bay compost system.

removable boards in the front of each bay. In the first bay build the heap with a layer of organic material such as grass cuttings and vegetable waste plus straw bedding. Tread down the heap and cover it with a thin layer of soil. Add lime if the soil pH is below 7, then water and continue the layers until the desired height is reached. Turn this heap

You can collect damaged windfall fruit, old vegetables and kitchen waste for composting.

every five to six weeks to speed up decomposition.

Cultivation of Soils

As discussed in Chapter 1, soil can be broken down into three types: clay, sandy and calcareous. The main aim when cultivating is to change each of these soil categories to create a uniform soil which will react to organic matter and provide good drainage and a good air supply.

Clay soils

These soils drain badly and initially they will need a drainage system. Changing clay soils takes time and you will also need to double dig the area to break up the top of the subsoil. Next you must concentrate on the surface layer. Digging should take place in the autumn to let the winter frosts work on the tilth. While digging apply an organic matter such as horse manure worked in with straw. This manure is low in moisture unlike pig and cow manure and ideal for a clay soil. Then apply an open material such

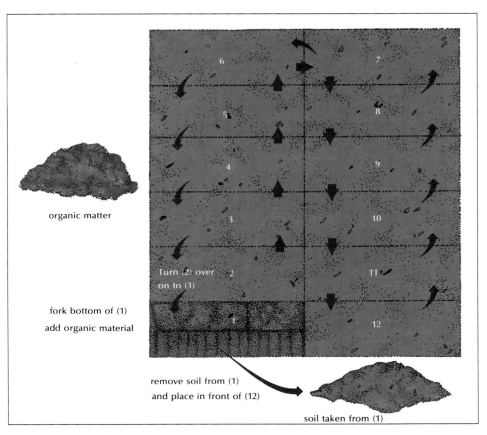

organic matter

Turn (2) over
on to (1)

fork bottom of (1)
add organic material

remove soil from (1)
and place in front of (12)

soil taken from (1)

A double digging plan.

as coarse sand and grit and mix it with the soil. Test the pH and if the level is below 6.5 apply ground limestone in the autumn. The rate of application depends on the pH level.

Sandy soil
Sandy soil drains too well so large amounts of manure high in nutrients (for example, pig and cow manure) are applied. To further help the nutrient level add a green manure every year. Potash is in short supply in these soils so you should also add wood

ash at about 4.5–9oz per sq yd (130–250g per sq m). Calcium will also be washed out so ground chalk can be added until the required pH level is reached. Cultivation of these soils can take place at any time, but early spring and late autumn are best.

Calcareous soils
These soils can be divided into chalk, limestone and clay marls. Treat clay marls like clay, but for the other two types dig over to break up the chalk and incorporate organic matter in the late autumn. Between spring

and autumn break any crust by lightly fork-ing or hoeing and cover the area with a well-rotted mulch of manure or tree bark – this helps to prevent a crust forming. Adding a green manure can be beneficial as can the addition of potassium in the form of burnt wood at 4.5–9oz per sq yd (130–250g per sq m).

Raised Beds

Raised beds are very useful if drainage is a problem, if you do not want to be bothered with heavy digging or if you want to create a new topsoil by buying in clean pest-, disease- and weed-free soil with a balanced pH level. If the bed is built on a worked soil, the old topsoil will become a culti-vated subsoil and it will also allow a greater depth for roots to penetrate.

Raised beds can be constructed with planks of wood (do not use railway sleepers as these have been coated with inorganic preservatives) or with a simple drystone wall (this is probably the best method) with soil placed between the gaps.

Start to build your raised bed by marking out the growing area and working out its height. The height will depend on the height of the water table – the higher the water table the higher the sides of the bed. Take into consideration the depth required by the roots – this will depend on which plants you intend to grow.

Weed Control

There are two main ways of controlling weeds depending on whether the land is cultivated or uncultivated. For cultivated land control the weeds as outlined below depending on what you intend to grow.

For vegetable patches remove all deep-rooted weeds during the autumn digging,

Apples
Apples need a balanced soil with good drainage, as some varieties are prone to diseases such as canker. Most apples crop better when planted in soil which allows for a deep root run of 6–8yd (2–4m).

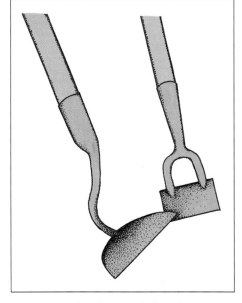

Two hoes used in the control of weeds.

Black plastic will help control weeds by stopping the light from reaching them.

then hand weed and hoe surface roots throughout the rest of the year. For tree and shrub beds hand weed and hoe throughout the growing season or cover the bed during this season with a mulch such as tree bark or with black plastic.

Mulching

Mulching helps to control weeds by blocking out the light so the weeds become leggy and weak or fail to grow at all. Any surface weeds in the mulch can easily be removed by hand. A 2in (5cm) layer should be spread over the area.

Black plastic

Good for the long-term growing area, black plastic stops the light from reaching the weeds. Cover up the plastic with a mulch layer such as tree bark and lay the plastic over land which has been cultivated in advance. Use a thick grade of plastic and lightly fork the ground surface before cover-

ing. Roll out the plastic and pin down the edges. Cut T shapes in the surface and dig holes ready to insert the plants. Secure the root systems of the plants into the soil, pull the plastic up to the stems and cover with the mulch.

On uncultivated land weed clearance can be hard work as the only sure way to clear the land is by hand. Decide on the plants you want to keep and those you do not. Cut all growth down to ground level, rake the area and collect the cuttings, sorting out those which can be composted as you go. The cut material can be spread over the area as a mulch. Buy a heavy-grade piece of black polythene and place it over the entire area to prevent the light from reaching the plants left in the soil. Leave the polythene in place until the plants under it have died back. Once the polythene has been removed, the land should be cultivated as described earlier.

3 • SEED SOWING AND PLANTING OUT

When establishing an organic garden the hardest task when growing the plants is that of controlling pests and disease without the use of artificial chemicals. The best way to avoid some of the troubles is to sow and germinate the seeds in trays and then transplant the seedlings into the soil later. This means that your plants get off to a good, clean start and, if you plan to transplant the seedlings around the life cycles of the main pests, you can also avoid attack while they are establishing themselves.

The compost used for seed sowing can be either organic compost which is useful for germinating and transplanting, or a mixture of horticultural sand and sterilized garden soil. Once the seeds have germinated do not move them before they have produced their first adult leaves. A compost for transplanting the germinated seeds into individual pots can contain 80 per cent sterilized garden soil and 20 per cent horticultural sand to which nutrients in the form of concentrated manures should be added.

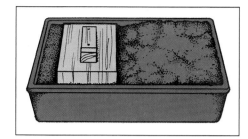

Seed tray and soil.

Sowing seeds.

Sowing Time

The sowing time depends on whether the plant is hardy or half-hardy – a hardy plant tolerates lower temperatures than a half-hardy one. Sow the seeds of most half-hardy and hardy annuals in tracks during early spring. However, sow brassicas later from September to January. Hardy seeds such as trees cannot be stored for long periods, and those that can will need a period of cold (stratification) before they will germinate.

Collecting and Growing Tree and Shrub Seeds

Many of these seeds grow directly in the soil, although some need stratification and others like oak do not store well and should be collected green and sown in the autumn.

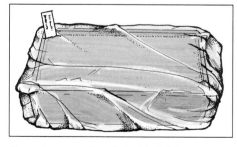

Cover the tray and mark the label giving the seed name and the date sown.

Seed can either be collected from the wild or bought from a garden centre. Bear in mind it is illegal to collect certain flower seed from the wild, so check first.

The time to collect seeds depends on when the tree or shrub flowers. In most cases this means that most are ready for collection from late summer to early autumn. It is important to collect the seeds before they ripen otherwise you will have to stratify them.

Stratification

This is the process that overcomes the dormancy period that sets in when seeds ripen. In order to stratify seeds obtain a seed tray with a depth of 3in (7.5cm) and drainage holes, and horticultural sand. Take one part of seed to three parts of sand, mix them together and fill the tray. Alternatively, spread a 1in (2.5cm) layer of peat substitute and sand mixture over the bottom of the seed tray. Place a layer of seeds on top and cover with a second layer of seed mixture. Continue this process until the tray is full.

Place the seed tray in a refrigerator set at a temperature of 30–40°F (1–4°C) for four to six weeks, or outside in a cold part of the garden, preferably north facing. Some exceptions such as *Berberis*, *Cotoneaster* and *Malus* will need a period of five to six months to stratify. Sow the seeds directly after stratification – usually from March to April.

Seed Sowing

Seeds can be sown on the surface of the compost and spread evenly. Small seeds can be left on the surface while larger seeds should be covered with a layer of compost sprinkled over the surface through a fine sieve.

Pricking Out

When the seeds have produced their first pair of adult leaves they can be transplanted into pots. Hold the seed by its leaves and push a flat dibber into the soil of the tray under the root system. Ease out the seedling

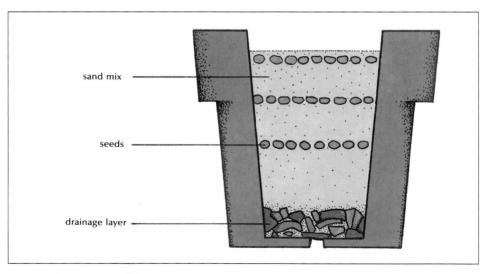

sand mix

seeds

drainage layer

Some seeds will need stratifying.

lift by holding
seed leaves and
pushing dibber
under seedlings

*Care should be taken when pricking out
so as not to damage the root system or
stem of a plant.*

and transfer it to the pot, positioning it so
that the seed leaves rest on top of the
compost. Leave as much soil around the
root system as possible when lifting the
seedling from the tray.

Guide to Sowing Times

As a guide to seed-sowing time I will take a
few examples of well-known plants as the
scope of this book does not run to a complete list.

Seeds sown in January–February
Rock gardens
Armeria; Aubretia; Cerastium.

Bulbs
Allium; Crocus; Hyacinthus; Iris; Muscari.

Herbaceous/bedding plants
Aquilegia; Dianthus; Phlox; Saxifraga.

Shrubs
Potentilla.

Seeds sown in March–May
Rock gardens
Acantholimon; Arabis; Pulmonaria.

Herbaceous/bedding plants
*Agapanthus; Alchemilla; Althaea; Alyssum;
Bellis; Bergenia; Borago; Calendula; Chrys-
anthemum; Delphinium; Dianthus; Digita-
lis; Euphorbia; Geum; Glaucium; Helian-
thus; Kniphofia; Leptospermum; Lobelia;
Lupinus; Matthiola; Mimulus; Myosotis;
Nicandra; Origanum; Primula x variablis;
Rodgersia; Salvia; Veronica; Viola.*

Shrubs
*Berberis; Buddleia; Buxus; Chaenomeles;
Cistus; Clematis; Cornus; Cotoneaster; Cyt-
isus; Genista; Helianthemum; Hibiscus;
Hydrangea; Hypericum; Laurus; Lonicera;
Mahonia; Pittosporum; Potentilla; Pyracan-
tha; Rhododendron; Rosa; Syringa; Wis-
teria.*

Strawberries
These prefer a well-drained soil. Buy certified
stock to avoid viral diseases. A net or cage is a
good idea to prevent birds eating the fruit.
Strawberries need extra feeding with
phosphates and potash to produce healthy
crops. The phosphates should be applied in
winter.

Trees
Acer; Betula; Cedrus; Crataegus; Ginko; Laburnum; Malus; Pinus; Prunus; Taxus; Thuja.

Seeds sown in September–October
Bulbs
Cardiocrinum.

Herbaceous bedding plants
Aconitum; Anemone; Delphinium; Lathyrus; Linaria; Nigella.

Trees
Aesculus; Castanea.

Planting

Planting in an organic garden is basically the same as for other types of gardening, in other words, the depth you dig depends upon the type of plant.

Trees Shrubs and Herbaceous Plants

Start by marking where the holes are to be dug – spacing is important so make sure you know the eventual height and spread of the plant and its roots. Dig the hole out with the soil placed at the sides. Push a fork into the sides of the hole to avoid smoothing it. Dig to the desired depth and width, and before planting fork the bottom of the hole and incorporate some well-rotted organic matter. Place the plant in the hole and spread out the root system. Before filling in the hole mix the soil with a small amount of well-rotted organic matter. Replace the soil, mixing it in between the root system by

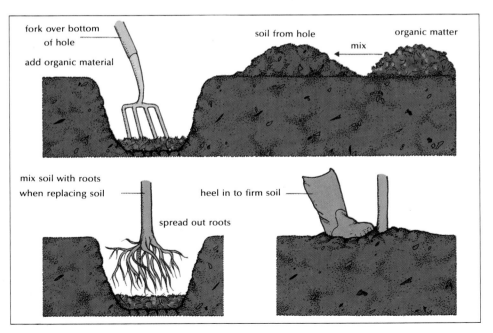

The technique of hole planting.

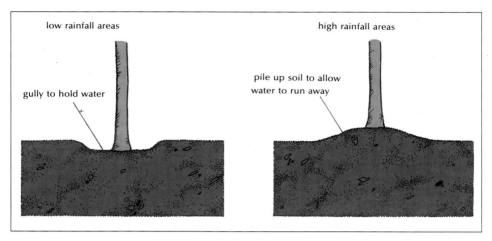

low rainfall areas

high rainfall areas

gully to hold water

pile up soil to allow
water to run away

Two ways of finishing off planting.

lifting the plant slightly by the stem and shaking it. Continue to fill the hole and firm down the soil with your heel. When you reach the top of the hole you can finish off the job either by leaving a gully around the plant – this is to hold water if you live in a fairly dry area – or by making a mound around the stem to drain the water away.

Trees will need a deep root run, but make sure the graft mark of those trees bottom worked (ie the graft is at the bottom of the tree) is not covered up. Although most trees are grafted at the bottom, some such as the small weeping varieties are grafted at the top (top worked).

Trees may need to be staked depending on their size and the wind speeds of the area. A strong wooden stake that will outlast the staking time of the tree (one to two years) is best. Tie the stake to the tree in two places – position one tie a third of the way up and position the other at the top. Check the tree regularly to make sure that the ties are not damaging the trunk.

Seeds

Cultivate the soil, feed it with top dressing such as dried blood, and bring it to a fine tilth after levelling it and removing large stones. Mark out the area for sowing. The depth and spacing of the seeds will be shown on the packet. Use a draw hoe and a wooden board to work on, form a drill and after planting your seed replace the soil and level it off.

Seedlings

When planting out seedlings the soil should be brought to a fine tilth as described earlier. Mark out the area and dig small holes to accommodate the root balls. Use a small hand trowel or fork for this. Plant and then water – the amount depends on the weather conditions. Seedlings that need protecting from frost can be covered with cloches and those that need protecting from birds can be covered with nets. Other forms of protection include the building of barriers and wind-breaks (*see* Chapter 6).

4 • FRUIT

When choosing fruit trees for the garden carefully study those varieties that are more resistant to pests and diseases, or rootstocks that are more immune to some forms of disease. Choosing these resistant types will help you as you obviously cannot use chemical insecticides or fungicides in your organic garden. There are even rootstocks that do well in poor soils – they will stand up better than others to natural elements when grown organically.

You will also need to gain a knowledge of flowering times for pollination and to avoid frost damage. Pruning is also important as it allows light and air to get to the centre of the plant and helps fight disease.

Tree Shapes

Most gardens these days are too small to grow large fruit trees let alone have room for an orchard, but it is possible to buy dwarf rootstock and grow the trees on these. They can be grown in several different shapes: cordons, espaliers, dwarf pyramids or small bush trees.

Fruit Cages

Again not many gardens have room for a large fruit cage, but if you do have room it will help control attacks from birds, act as a wind-break, protect plants from frost and give shade from very hot, sunny weather. You can obtain small fruit cages, for example, wall fruit cages which can be erected around trees grown against a wall. These will only protect trees grown against a wall from attack by birds. Other small varieties are available to protect say, a few dwarf types, or you could construct your own cage.

A well laid out and planned fruit and vegetable garden will make planting and tending easier.

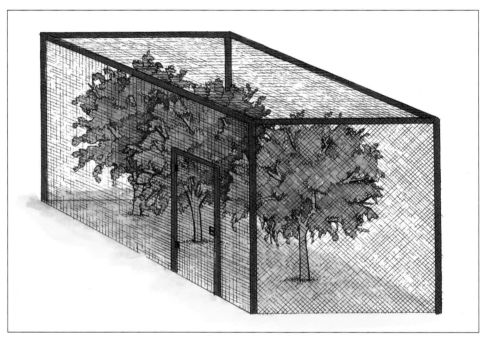

A free-standing fruit cage.

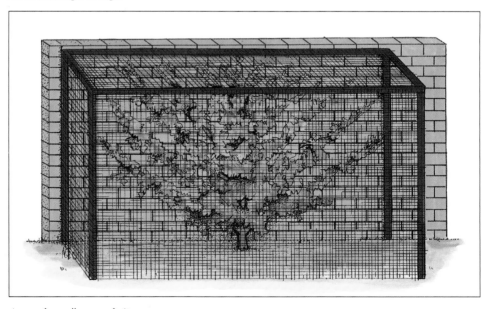

A cage for wall-grown fruit.

Soil

The main fruit trees – apple, pear, plum and cherries – are suited to deep cultivation with organic matter and do particularly well with raised beds, although some cherries prefer grassed areas to a cultivated top soil.

Planting

Remember that the area where the rootstock and the top section (bud or scion) join should not be buried in the soil. If this happens the scion may take root and you will end up with a larger tree and no fruit.

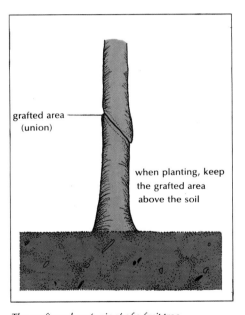

grafted area
(union)

when planting, keep
the grafted area
above the soil

The graft mark or 'union' of a fruit tree.

Spacing

This depends on the type of rootstock (either dwarf or vigorous) and the style of tree. Remember to find out the eventual

Plums
Plums and gages need the same kind of soil and planting conditions as apples and pears. As with most plants, some are more susceptible than others to attacks from disease and infections, and the old favourite 'Victoria' (above) tends to be more vulnerable than most.

height and spread of the tree before planting as you do not want an overcrowded area.

Pruning

Once you have worked over your soil and chosen the rootstock you need, then you will have to consider pruning. If you leave stumps to rot and branches to rub against each other you will stop light and air from circulating around the plant and leave them susceptible to disease. It is important to remove dead, damaged and diseased wood and then follow this by removing any crossing branches. Once you have taken these out very little other pruning is needed. There are forms of pruning such as spur and renewal pruning, and there are cosmetic prunings which allow in light and air to the centre of the plant – these are covered on pages 30–33.

Dead Wood

This is an excellent breeding ground for disease and it will not take long for insects to start burrowing into the soft, decaying wood. There they will build nests and lay eggs so that future generations will hatch out and infect your tree by colonizing other areas. The insects can also transfer to other healthy plants growing nearby. You must therefore cut off dead sections as soon as possible making sure not to leave stumps that will die back.

Damaged Wood

A damaged branch may still show signs of healthy life, but sooner or later a disease will enter the tree through this section. It is here that you should practise preventive pruning.

Diseased Wood

Diseases such as canker and coral spot must be removed by pruning as soon as they are discovered.

Crossing Branches

Branches which are allowed to cross one another will eventually rub in strong winds, thereby damaging themselves and allowing disease to enter the tree. Remove these branches during the annual pruning.

It is worth remembering that you should not leave old, pruned wood lying about as it may spread disease. Do not compost it or burn it for recycling as wood ash as this may well reinfect the whole area. Always keep piles of wood ready for burning away from growing areas to avoid the danger of pests

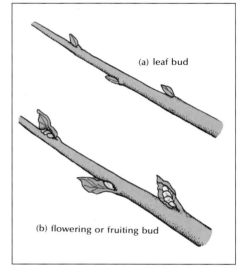

The leaf bud tends to be flat against the wood (a). Flowering buds are cigar-shaped (b).

breeding and overwintering. Old canes should be treated in the same way as their hollow stems offer ideal housing for over-wintering insects.

How to Prune

Cutting to the correct position and the right angle is a very important factor when growing plants organically. The angle is important as it allows water to run away from the wound or bud. On some fruit such as apples and pears it is important to know the difference between a leaf bud and a flowering bud. A leaf bud lies flat against the branch while a flowering one is cigar shaped.

Pruning for Spurs

A spur is a small group of flowering buds growing from a sub-branch of a side branch (lateral). Spurs found on fruit trees are

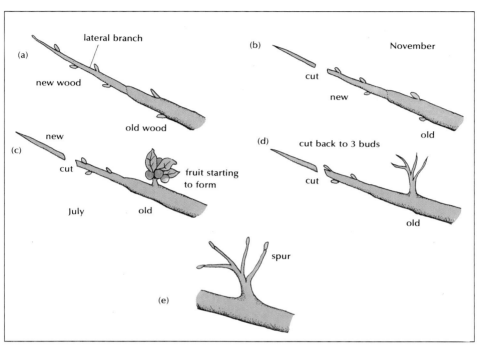

(a) By pruning the growing tips, lateral branches further down the tree will be encouraged to grow. (b) and (c) Large cigar-shaped buds are those which produce flowers and these in turn produce fruit when pollinated. (d) Avoid leaving stumps. (e) Spurs are produced on old wood.

encouraged through pruning. They produce an abundance of flowering buds and if these are pollinated they will give a good fruit crop. The spur forms on the second year's wood after the first year's growth is cut back in November – cutting back to two or three buds encourages lateral growth. After this stage pruning takes place twice a year during November and in July when the fruit is starting to form. The summer pruning helps to form the spur and lets light and air reach the developing fruit.

Spur thinning
After several years the spur will become too crowded and the fruit will have to compete for space, light and air, thus resulting in a poor crop. At this time you should thin out the spur by spacing it out to just a few sub-branches. It is best to carry out this thinning before the fruit is formed, ie in the autumn, as this cuts down the work required.

Thinning fruit
When the young fruits first form some will fall from the tree – this is called 'June drop' and is a natural process as the tree is trying to thin out its own crop. If after this process the crop is still too crowded you will have to thin it out as well. You can leave one to three fruits in a section of the spur, but if two fruits are touching, one or more should be removed with a pair of sharp secateurs or long-handled scissors.

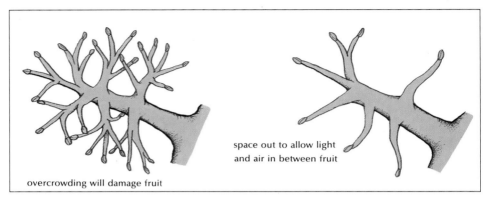

Spur training – spurs will need thinning to prevent the fruit from becoming overcrowded.

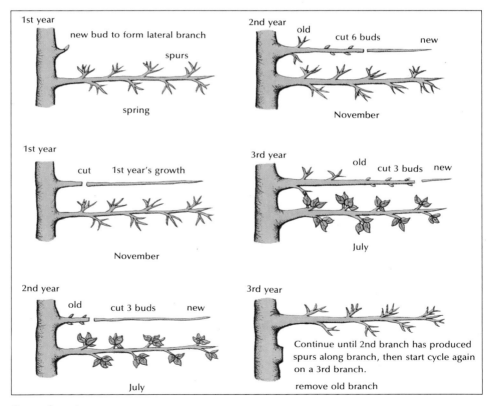

Renewal pruning.

Renewal Pruning

For a maximum crop combine spur pruning on the older section of the tree with renewal pruning on the new growth. This is similar to spur pruning but the fruit is produced on a long spur. After three years the complete branch is removed to encourage healthy new growth.

The scope of this book does not allow great detail on all the different types of fruit trees that are available, but we can look at some of the aspects of growing these plants organically.

Apples

Apples are grown organically in the same way as they are grown inorganically, but the conditions for organic growth should be as perfect as possible as the tree will need to be more vigorous than inorganically grown ones. You will have to create a natural balance between tree and soil, and combine a study of pest and disease life cycles and resistant rootstocks. You will also need to take some cosmetic measures, for example, removing scab by pruning, or choosing a scab-resistant tree such as 'Egremont Russet'.

Always wait until you have a balanced soil with good drainage before growing apples as some varieties such as 'Cox's Orange Pippin' are prone to diseases such as canker. You will find that most apples crop better when planted in soil which allows for a deep root run of 6–13ft (2–4m), so they are ideal for raised beds.

Pollination and Flowering Times

Apples, and for that matter cherries and plums, will not produce a proper crop unless they are cross-pollinated with a compatible variety. You must therefore buy trees that flower at the same time and which are

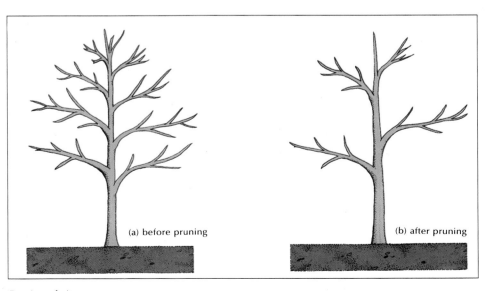

(a) before pruning

(b) after pruning

Pruning a fruit tree.

Some branches will need support to take the weight of the tree.

from the same group of trees or groups that overlap. If you do not do this pollination cannot take place. Whether a tree is biennial or triploid will also affect pollination (*see* below).

Weather Conditions

If you live in an area prone to late frost it is best to choose apples which are late flowering, such as those from Group 3 or 4 on page 35.

Apple Groups

There are three main types of apple tree: diploid, triploid and biennial. The best ones to cultivate first are diploid trees as the other two have certain problems attached to them.

Biennial trees

These fruit trees can miss a flowering period one year, then flower the next, so do not use them as a pollinator of other trees. To ensure pollination plant two other non-biennial trees from the same group or an overlapping group. If you already have these types of tree or are thinking of planting them, seek further advice from a local nursery.

Triploid trees

Most apple trees are diploid which means that they contain the usual number of chromosomes. However, some are termed triploid and these have 1.5 times the usual number of chromosomes in the nuclei of their cells. If you grow two trees of this type together poor pollination will result – instead plant one triploid tree with two diploid ones. Again seek further advice before purchasing these types.

General diploid groups

There are many trees in these groups but I will mention a few of the more common ones here as a guide.

Group 1
An early flowering group – if you are just starting out it is best to avoid this group and go for a later flowering group, unless you have a sheltered garden. Examples: 'Lord Suffield'; 'Red Astrachan'.

Group 2
Another early flowering group. Examples: 'Beauty of Bath'; 'Egremont Russet'; 'Laxton's Early Crimson'; 'Lord Lambourne'; 'Norfolk Beauty'.

Group 3
The largest and best group to start with to avoid frost damage. Examples: 'Cox's Orange Pippin'; 'Discovery'; 'Granny Smith'; 'Jonathan'; 'Merton Russet'; 'Merton Worcester'; 'Spartan'; 'Worcester Pearmain'.

Group 4
Later flowering than group three and a good group to start with. Examples: 'Delicious'; 'Golden Delicious'; 'Laxton's Pearmain'; 'Lord Derby'.

Group 5
'Merton Beauty'; 'Newton Wonder'; 'Royal Jubilee'.

Group 6
'Bess Pool'; 'Edward VII'; 'Laxton's Royalty'.

Group 7
'Crawley Beauty' – this one will set fruit without cross-pollination in the right conditions.

Rootstocks

Rootstocks have been produced through many years of research. They help the organic fruit grower as they give more control over size and vigour of growth, they can often be used to counteract poor soil, and many have been developed to help fight pest and disease. Rootstocks change all the time as new ones are found and old ones discarded. You should consult your nursery and give them your requirements before purchasing, or alternatively contact the Ministry of Agriculture for up-to-date information.

Cherries

There are two kinds of cherry – sweet and acid – both of which like a well-balanced soil with plenty of depth. The sweet cherry dislikes cultivation around the surface area of its root system as this could cause gummosis – instead plant this tree in uncultivated ground with grass around the roots.

Sweet Cherry

This is not a tree for the small garden and it grows best in groups. It will not set fruit unless pollinated by other cherries. These trees need a grass covering around their roots, so plant a hard-wearing perennial type like ryegrass and allow clover to take hold as its nitrogen content is useful.

Acid Cherries

The fruit is mainly used for cooking and the tree can be grown against a wall. They can be grown as a single tree or as a bush.

Flowering Times

There are five groups of cherry – some are self-compatible and set fruit on their own but may give a poor crop, while there are those that need several trees to pollinate each other. This book is not large enough to list all cherry groups so below is a list of the most popular trees and those which are best to grow.

Sweet cherries
'Early Rivers' – fruits in late June, plant with 'Merton Favourite' for pollination. 'Merton Favourite' – fruits in July; plant with 'Early Rivers'.

Acid cherries
'Morello' – self-compatible, the fruit is ready in August and the tree is ideal for planting against a wall.

Rootstock

Careful choice of rootstock will help you fight pests and disease, for example, Malling F12/1 is good for resistance to bacterial canker. As with apples, seek advice from local nurseries before buying.

If the cherry tree needs to be grassed down after planting, cultivate the land as described in Chapter 7 and bring it to a fine tilth before sowing the grass seed.

With organic gardening healthy soft fruit can be obtained to reward all the effort.

Other Forms of Fruit

Soft summer fruit bushes are numerous, so just a few varieties are discussed with information given on suggested soil, mulching and pruning.

Blackberries

The information given for this fruit is also relevant for loganberries and boysenberries. The soil should be well balanced and cultivated with good drainage, yet retaining moisture. Blackberries benefit from a deep root run, so raised beds are ideal.

Mulching should be with well-rotted straw compost containing manure. This will benefit the plant and help with weed control and moisture retention.

After planting out, cut the plants down to 9in (23cm) off the ground. Tie new growth to training wires which should be 12–14in (30–35cm) apart as this will allow light and air to reach the centre and will help to prevent fungal diseases. Fruit is produced on the older stems so keep the new growth separate from the old when training. Cut the old growth after fruiting and then move the new growth to replace it, so giving space for further growth.

Raspberries

Only buy Ministry of Agriculture certified plants as these will be clean plants, free from disease. The raspberry likes plenty of organic matter and a deep cultivated soil. They should be planted in rows with each cane about 18in (46cm) apart.

The fruiting season can be either summer or autumn but the autumn-fruiting raspberries tend to produce a smaller crop, so if you choose the right varieties you can have fruit over several months. Summer fruit is produced on the previous year's wood while autumn fruit is produced on the current season's wood. In both cases cut back

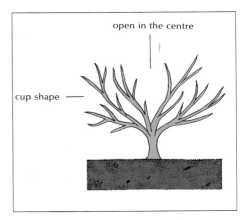

Prune to allow light and air to enter the centre of the bush.

the cane to 9in (23cm) after planting out and do not allow the plant to fruit in its first year.

For summer raspberry pruning cut the canes down to ground level after fruiting and tie in new growth 3in (8cm) apart to allow air circulation and light penetration. Make sure that you remove all suckers from the rows to stop overcrowding as this creates conditions for disease. Cut back the top growth of each cane about 5in (13cm) in the early spring – if you do this earlier you will take away protection from bad weather and frost.

Autumn raspberries should be cut down to 6in (15cm) above ground in February or March.

Black Currants

These are ideal for the organic garden, but do not allow the plants to fruit in their first year, and ensure that you allow light and air to reach the centre of the plant in order to control disease. The soil should be mulched throughout the growing season with well-rotted compost containing manure and straw.

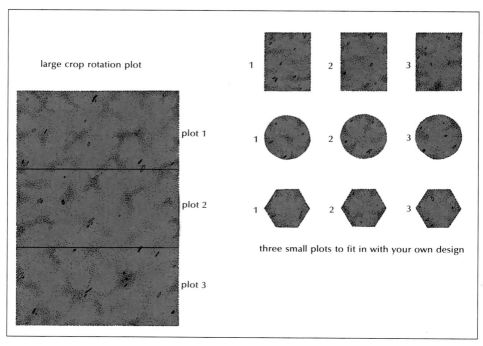

large crop rotation plot

1 2 3

plot 1 — 1 2 3

plot 2

1 2 3

three small plots to fit in with your own design

plot 3

Crop rotation will prevent the build-up of pests and disease.

After planting out, cut the plants back by 1–1.5in (2–3cm), and cut the bush into a cup shape to allow light and air into the centre of the plant. In the autumn of the first year cut down the weak shoots so that stronger ones are produced that will fruit the following year. Annual pruning is undertaken to cut back the older wood after you have picked the crop.

Gooseberries

These need a deep-cultivated soil with ample drainage and organic matter. Gooseberries will need feeding with potash in March – the rate depends on how much is already in your soil. You should also mulch the area to control weeds.

Gooseberries should be pruned in winter

and summer. Winter prune bushes over two years old and try to maintain an open cup shape (as for blackcurrants) to allow light and air penetration. Remove any dead, damaged or diseased branches, then remove any crossed and rubbing branches. Next cut the healthy branches back by half to an outward facing bud. Cut back side shoots to three buds as this will encourage spurs. Summer pruning takes place at the end of June when you can cut back the side growth to four or five leaves.

Strawberries

Again, this fruit prefers a well-drained soil containing plenty of organic matter. Buy certified stock to avoid viral diseases. If you do not have room for a fruit cage and you

The fruit of strawberries should be kept off the soil with the use of straw bedding.

plan to grow the strawberry plants in the open, net them to prevent birds eating the fruit. Cloches can be used to protect one-year-old plants and to keep off the birds. Use mulching straw around the neck of the plant and outward to support the fruit and act as a weed control. You could use plastic mats or black polythene instead, but you would lose the organic benefits of recycled straw. The surrounding area can be covered with black polythene to cut out light and control the weeds.

Strawberries need extra feeding with phosphates and potash to produce healthy fruit, although little extra nitrogen is needed. Remember to apply the phosphates in winter.

STRAWBERRY VARIETIES
Cambridge Prizewinner   Early season
Royal Sovereign   Early season
Cambridge Favourite   Mid-season, good
   for first year crop, plant July/August.
Talisman   Mid-season
Rabunda   Late season.

5 • VEGETABLES

As with fruit, it is important to choose plant varieties that are resistant or immune to disease as you will have a battle on your hands once the plants start to grow. What you must remember is that your organic vegetables are not always going to be lush, green, perfect specimens. They will have blemishes as a result of pests and diseases, but this is only a cosmetic drawback and by growing them you will cause yourself and the environment less damage than if you produced an artificially perfect specimen.

If you start by making sure your vegetable plot has good drainage, this will prevent a multitude of problems. With good drainage you will have a warm soil earlier in the year than if your soil had poor drainage, and this

Good looking carrots grown without the aid of artificial chemicals.

Onions
These prefer a light, well-drained soil. Heavy, wet soil encourages soft bulbs which are difficult to store. White rot fungus is likely to cause problems.

will encourage earlier germination of seeds. Increased air flow and the temperature of well-drained soil is also important to seedlings at the transplanting stage. Bacterial activity in well-drained soil is encouraged, and this allows organic matter breakdown to be accelerated. Cultivation can therefore take place earlier in the year, even after heavy rainfall.

Weather Protection

Frost and wind are the two main weather problems for vegetables, but heavy rain and

Make sure you plant vegetables with enough room for them to grow without overcrowding.
If there is not much space in the garden incorporate vegetables in the flower beds.

Vegetables like peas and beans can be grown up trellis if there is not room for a row of canes.

Planting in rows allows for easier access.

hailstorms can also cause damage. Avoid planting in a known frost pocket and erect wind-breaks (*see* Chapter 6).

Growing Under Glass

Crops can be produced under glass during the winter if good soil cultivation and drainage procedures have been followed. However, you will probably have to heat the greenhouse and the cost of this may well be prohibitive, especially on a large scale.

Raised Beds

This system is a good way of overcoming drainage problems, especially if you have a clay soil. You can have one large bed or

Raised beds are the ideal kind for creating a vegetable area quickly.

Healthy leeks can be grown in well-dug and organically treated soil as they particularly like well-rotted compost.

several small ones, but whichever one you choose remember that you will have to practise a form of crop rotation if you want to grow vegetables every year. Therefore, if you opt for a number of beds make sure you have either three or four.

Crop Rotation

The aim of a three-plot crop rotation is to grow a different type of crop in each plot on a three-year cycle. If you have a four-plot system the procedure is basically the same, but the fourth bed is kept empty for general cultivation and weed control. You could also plant this fourth bed with a green manure such as mustard seed if it is big enough.

The idea of the rotation system is one of the basic historical forms of agriculture and vegetable gardening, and the system has not changed as it works very well. It prevents the build-up of soil pests on all the plots, and by cultivating the soil with deep-rooted crops and feeding it with different nutrients depending on the different crops, a build-up over the years of one particular nutrient is avoided.

Growing brassicas in one bed as part of crop rotation on a plot.

Crop/plot 1: year 1

Peas, beans and salad vegetables. Peas are ideal for they have nitrogen-fixing properties. Test the soil for levels of nitrogen before adding extra organic fertilizer.

Crop/plot 2: year 1

After testing the soil for nutrient levels dress it with organic fertilizer such as dried blood, bonemeal and wood ash if necessary. Plant all forms of root crop.

Crop/plot 3: year 1

Grow all forms of brassica in this plot. They need a neutral pH, so test the soil first and adjust it by adding lime if necessary.

During the second and third years move up one plot. For example, the crop in plot one is planted in plot two during the second

Help to ripen tomatoes by placing in a sunny spot.

First Step

Make sure that you have a good, working drainage system, that the soil is cultivated and the pH level as close as possible to 6.5–7. You can build raised beds for better drainage and a deeper soil if you prefer.

Second Step

Double dig the area leaving the surface in lumps so that the frost can break it up over the winter. In the spring lightly fork and rake the area into a fine tilth for sowing or transplantation.

Third Step

During the winter plan your three-year crop rotation.

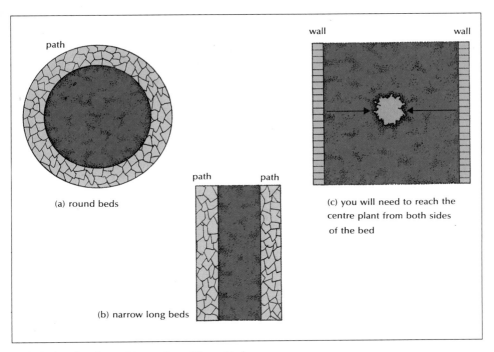

(a) round beds

(b) narrow long beds

(c) you will need to reach the centre plant from both sides of the bed

Beds designed so that walking on the soil is avoided.

year, plot two becomes plot three and plot three becomes plot one – this process then continues on a three-year cycle.

Non-Dig System

When carrying out this system you must never walk on the soil to prevent it from becoming compacted. By following this rule, double digging is avoided and earthworms are allowed to do most of the work.

For the non-dig system you will need narrow, raised beds in either a rectangular, circular or square shape. You must be able to reach the centre of the bed from at least two sides, so take this into consideration when building the beds. Here again, drainage and cultivation are very important as is

the correct neutral pH level. All these factors will give the area the right conditions to allow the soil organisms to do the work for you.

Close Planting

A system whereby the crop is planted without .any spacing to create an umbrella which will help stop weed growth and prevent soil damage. You must, however, watch out for a build-up of disease through lack of air flow with this system. Some of the foliage may also show signs of poor growth through lack of light, and you must water carefully to prevent some plants drying out due to the increased competition.

6 • PESTS, DISEASES AND WEATHER PROTECTION

The first part of this chapter looks at suggestions for coping with adverse weather conditions. If you follow these suggestions they will help counteract die-back caused by frost and damage from strong winds. Hygiene also plays a part in maintaining healthy plants as well as pruning. Pruning allows air to circulate around a plant and therefore helps prevent the build-up of moulds thus eliminating the need for chemical fungicides. The organic gardener must also study the life cycles of common pests as this will give an indication of when and where they breed. By getting the sowing time correct, knowing where the pests hide on the plant, how to find their nests, and where their breeding and hibernation areas are, you can eliminate them without using any form of insecticide.

Protection from Adverse Weather

Frost

All plants will be damaged if attacked by frost – the signs of this are when young shoots are scorched and turn black. Frost

Use straw as a form of protection around the plants against adverse weather.

damage in turn can give rise to diseases such as canker. There are two kinds of frost – air frost and ground frost – and they are most destructive in spring and autumn.

Spring frosts
Spring frosts are the most damaging to seedlings and plants in general. The moisture inside the plant cells turns into ice crystals in a frost and most of the damage is caused when these ice crystals warm up too quickly in the sun. It can therefore be

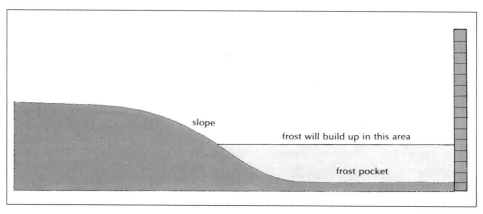

slope

frost will build up in this area

frost pocket

Avoid growing plants in frost pockets.

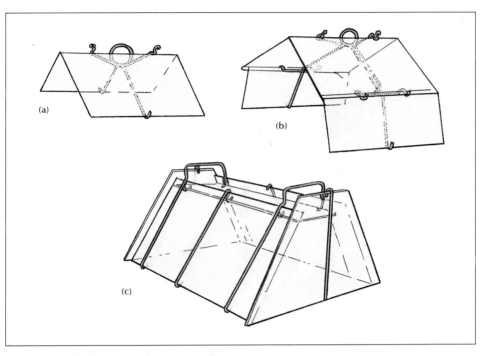

Types of glass cloche. (a) Tent (b) Barn (c) Utility or tomato.

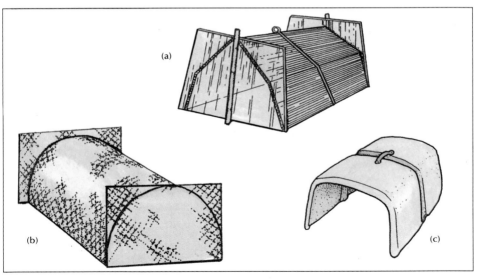

Types of plastic cloche. (a) Polypropylene (semi-rigid, double layered)
(b) Wire-reinforced plastic (c) Polystyrene (rigid plastic).

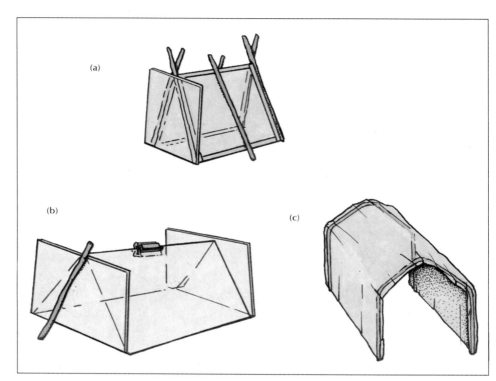

Home-made cloches: (a) Tent cloche protection over young bean plants, made by attaching polythene film to battens and securing them to the bean poles up which the beans later climb. (b) Odd panes of glass made into cloches with Rumsey clips. (c) Low cloches made from plastic bags and coat hangers; use rigid glass or rigid plastic for end pieces.

helpful to spray plants with cold water to slow down the warm-up period so causing less damage. Spray the plants before 10 a.m. as this will also avoid sun-scorch which is a result of water droplets magnifying the sun's rays.

Spring frost can occur at any time between March and May, a time when buds and shoots are at their most vulnerable. Most of these frosts are ground frosts and are penetrating. The frost moves down a slope like running water, so never position plants, cold frames or glasshouses at the bottom of a slope.

Autumn frost

Autumn frost is not quite as damaging as spring frost, especially for trees and shrubs as they have usually entered their dormant period and so contain less moisture which can form ice crystals. Damage often occurs when frost is combined with a strong wind.

Wind

Wind can have a drying effect on the soil or on seed compost, and on the woody section, foliage and root systems of plants — it can be fatal as the entire moisture content of

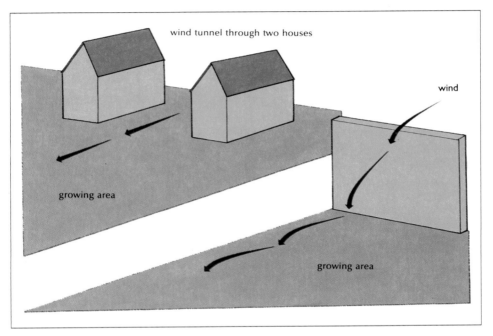

Avoid wind tunnels and turbulence caused by walls and fences.

a plant can dry out in the matter of a few hours in a windy position. In windy conditions the plant compensates for the loss of moisture by drawing up more moisture through its root system, and the faster the wind speed the more the plant will do this. At the same time, however, the wind is drying out the soil thus leaving the plant without water and causing it to wilt.

Local winds or turbulence can also be caused by the following structures, so be careful when positioning your planting beds.

Houses

Two houses positioned close together can form a wind tunnel with very high-speed winds; corners of houses may also have the same effect. Do not position your bed at the end of one of these tunnels.

Walls

Solid walls also cause turbulence. The area of turbulence is not directly underneath the wall but a few feet from the wall. Check out the area where most damage could be caused by hanging flags on canes – position your plant bed accordingly. If you are going to build a wall make it an 'open' type to filter the wind.

Fences

Again, open fences are better than solid ones as they filter the wind. Note, however, that wooden fences also provide a haven for overwintering pests.

Wind-breaks

There are several forms of wind-break.

Natural wind-breaks Natural forms of wind-break allow the wind to filter through,

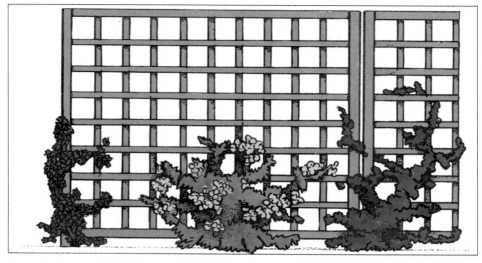

A wooden framework will offer protection by filtering the wind.

thus preventing turbulence. The best form of wind-break is a hedge such as conifer, hawthorn, beech or privet. However, do make sure that you do not let the hedge shade the plant beds.

Netting Plastic netting with small-grade mesh can be bought from garden centres and acts as a good wind-break.

Fruit cages These make good wind-breaks and protect against some pests and frost.

Cold frames These give ideal protection as well as being important for starting seeds, growing cuttings and hardening off plants. They can also provide protection against some pests such as carrot root fly – this works if the barrier is 3ft (1m) high and encloses the carrot seedlings. Aluminium cold frames with their tops removed are ideal for the framework. They can be fitted with glass or heavy grade polythene. You can move the frame easily from year to year so that the carrots do not have to be planted in the same place.

Pests

Damage by specific insects and other closely related species is one form of pest attack. The damage is usually caused by caterpillars of various moths and butterflies, by the adults and grubs of some beetles; by weevils and by the maggots of tiny flies.

There are also pests which live in the soil, for example, millipedes, cutworms, wireworms and leather-jackets. Pests which attack above ground are night-feeding slugs and snails which feed on plants by biting their leaves, stems and roots.

There is also the group of sap-sucking insects such as aphids (greenfly and blackfly) which cause the leaves to be distorted, twisted, curled or blistered. Aphids are particularly bad as they often transmit viral diseases in the process. Finally, pests include larger animals such as mice, moles, rabbits, cats, dogs and birds. The larger of these animals can be deterred by the use of cold frames, netting or cloches.

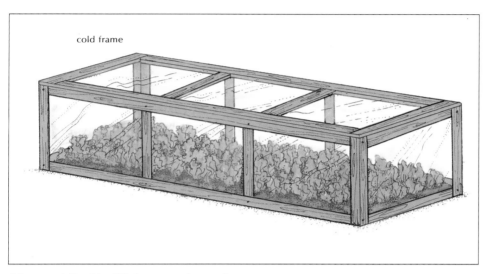

cold frame

A framework like this will help to control carrot fly.

Vegetables and fruit can be protected from birds and small mammals by covering with netting.

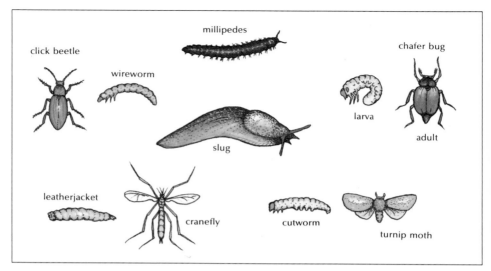

Soil Pests.

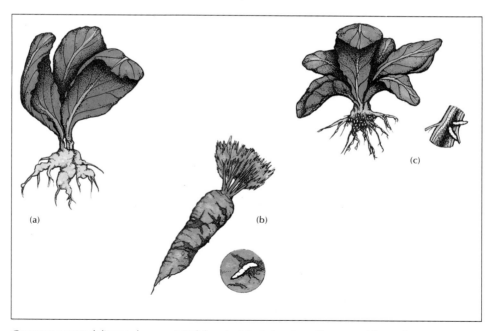

Common pest and disease damage. (a) Clubroot: distorted root swellings on cabbage plant caused by clubroot fungus. (b) Carrot fly: carrot root tunnelled by tiny maggots, about ⅕in (0.5cm) long which cause severe damage. (c) Cabbage root fly: young plant severely damaged by cabbage root fly maggot. Infected plants wilt and die.

Companion planting can help control some forms of pest attack.

Growing plants close together can help choke weeds but has other drawbacks.

Diseases

Diseases that affect vegetables can be divided into two groups. The first includes those caused by fungi, bacteria and viruses. Fungi are usually visible to the naked eye, but with bacteria and viruses you only see the results of their attack.

Fungi and bacteria cause greyish moulds and mildews on leaves, clubroot gall in brassicas, various rots that attack onions and damping-off diseases that affect seedlings. Viral diseases are very difficult to control and if you suspect your plant is suffering from this type of disease it is better to pull it up and burn it to prevent a spread of the infection.

The second group of diseases contains those which are a symptom of poor growing conditions, for example, incorrect temperature, lack of water or poor soil conditions.

All diseases are more difficult to cure and control for the organic gardener than pests,

and in most cases by the time you have recognized the disease it is too late, so prevention is better and easier than cure. In all the above cases these groups of disease are preventable, and if you follow the advice given in this book they should not even arise.

Preventative Measures

Most pests and diseases can be avoided or minimized by organic gardeners if the soil is balanced as described in the first two chapters of this book. Once this has been done

Growing vegetables under glass can give you more control over the environment for organic gardening.

you can look at other preventative measures such as garden hygiene.

Garden Hygiene

At some stage during their life cycle many common pests depend on rubbish lying about in the garden or weeds to protect them. If you remove these on a regular basis you will therefore help to keep the pests at bay. For example: aphids hide in brassicas during the winter and in late spring produce a winged generation which flies off to infect another victim; the flea beetle overwinters in weeds; slugs hide in sheltered spots such

Tomatoes
Tomatoes require a deep soil, well supplied with organic matter. Best sown in the greenhouse, they can be transplanted when a good root system has developed. Potato blight is one of the main diseases to watch for.

as rubbish or bits of rotten wood; a viral disease that attacks lettuce plants overwinters in weed seeds such as chickweed; and weeds also harbour cabbage root fly, blackfly and clubroot fungus. It is therefore important to keep your garden clean and tidy by clearing out old plants such as winter brassicas by mid-May keeping weeds down and clearing out all potential hiding places for pests, for example, old leaves under hedges and debris in the bottom of ditches.

Other pests and diseases can be kept at bay by sowing seeds in a seed tray which can be controlled before the established seedlings are planted out, and by rotating the crops as discussed in Chapter 5 (*see* page 43). Overcrowding your plants will create another danger area as air will not be able to circulate and fungal diseases may spread rapidly. Overcrowded plants will also have to compete for water and nutrients and may become weak and less resistant as a result.

By studying the life cycle of some of the pests you can avoid attack by varying the sowing or planting out time of seedlings. For example, broad beans sown in autumn and early spring will escape the worst of blackfly; turnips sown in June will escape flea beetle attack, and onions grown in sets rather than from seed will escape damage from the onion fly. Companion planting often works as a deterrent as well. For example, planting French marigolds between tomato and pepper plants which are grown under cover seems to lessen whitefly attack. Another example of planting for protection is if when growing tomatoes and potatoes outside, you plant the tomatoes as far as possible from the potatoes to cut down the risk of potato blight.

If there is the space, well laid out rows of plants will help control some diseases and pest attacks.

Resistant rootstocks in fruit trees and seeds are being developed all the time by breeding cultivars, so you should keep your eyes open for these types as they will help you in your fight to keep plants healthy.

Safe Pesticides

There are some pesticides that are approved for use by organic gardeners. They are mainly derived from plants and break down rapidly into harmless products so no harmful residue is left in the soil. Generally they do not affect beneficial insects. The draw-

---

Safe pesticides and fungicides

Derris   Harmless to bees and hoverfly larvae, but harmful to fish. Effective against aphids, caterpillars and red spider mite in liquid form and against flea beetle in dust form.

Pyrethrum   Not harmful to natural predators or bees. More effective if mixed with derris. Effective against aphids, caterpillars and flea beetle.

Nicotine   Available as 2 per cent nicotine soap and harmless to predators, but kills bees so spray in the evening. Poisonous to mammals, so do not eat sprayed plants for forty-eight hours. Always wear gloves when spraying. Effective against aphids, mealy bugs, most caterpillars, pea and bean weevils, red spider mite and thrips.

Home-made rhubarb spray   Make by chopping up 3lb (1.4kg) of rhubarb leaves, boil for half an hour in 6pt (3.4 litres) of water, strain off and leave to cool. Dissolve 1oz (30g) of soap-flakes in 2pt (1.1 litres) of water, mix with the rhubarb liquid and spray. Effective against aphids.

Bordeaux mixture   A general fungicide in either a liquid or dust form, and made of copper sulphate and quicklime. A preventive spray for potatoes and tomatoes against potato blight.

Fertosan slug killer   Harmless to mammals, birds and earthworms, will keep ground free of slugs and snails for several months. It must not be sprayed on to seedlings and leaves in dry conditions.

---

back is that they are not as powerful as chemical pesticides and so their effectiveness is short lived. However, they are ideal for small gardens where you are not likely to have a large area planted out.

Biological Control

In some cases the natural enemies of a pest or disease can be harnessed to control it. This avoids the use of chemicals, and avoids damage to the environment and beneficial insects. There are difficulties in applying a biological control, but three examples have been tried and tested for use by the organic gardener: cabbage caterpillar can be controlled with the bacterial spray thuricide which can be used out of doors; whitefly can be controlled in greenhouses with the parasite *Encarsia formosa*; and red spider mite can also be controlled in greenhouses with the predator *Phytoseiulus persimilis*.

Greasebands

These are used mainly for fruit trees. Cut a

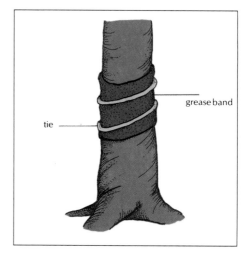

Greasebands.

piece of cloth big enough to go round the trunk of the tree, then fasten it to the trunk and cover it with medical jelly. As the insect makes its way up the trunk to hibernate for the winter it becomes stuck in the greaseband and can then be removed by hand.

Alternative Measures for Pest Control

Insect pests
Aphids Keep the plants well watered as attacks are less frequent on turgid plants. Collect ladybirds and move them to the infested plant as they feed on aphids. Squash the colonies by hand.

Cabbage root fly Prevent the adult fly from laying eggs by protecting the stem of newly transplanted plants with a physical

Pick off caterpillars.

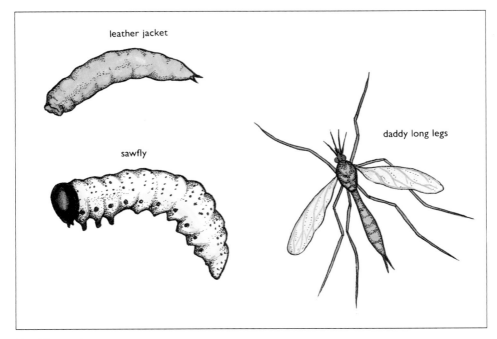

Troublesome insects.

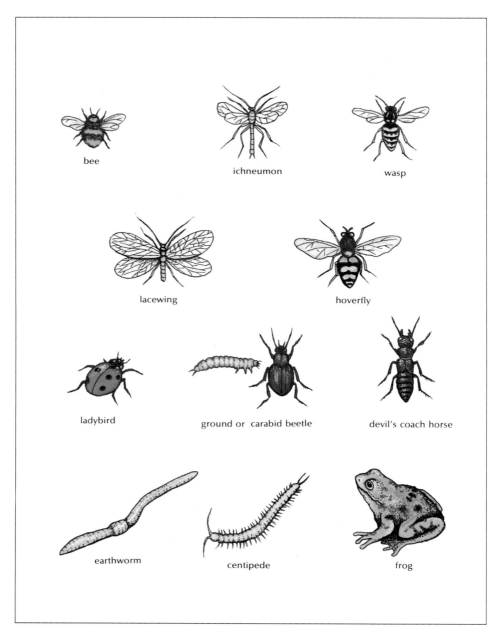

Some beneficial insects and other creatures.

barrier such as a 6in (15cm) diameter disc of carpet foam underlay. A plastic yoghurt pot can be used as a protective collar: make a hole in the bottom of the pot large enough to slip the cabbage root through from above, plant the root and bury the pot rim about 0.5in (1cm) deep in the soil.

Carrot fly Surround the carrot bed with a barrier of heavy-duty polythene at least 18in (45cm) high and buried 2in (5cm) deep in the soil.

Caterpillars Pick them off by hand.

Soil pests

Slugs and snails Hunt them down at night with a torch to catch them feeding. Collect them in pots or buckets and pour boiling water over them. In the day track them down to their hiding places under wood or boards. Slugs can also be caught with traps made of containers sunk in the ground and then filled with beer, however, this method also catches beneficial beetles.

Other soil pests Regular digging and hoeing will expose other soil pests such as millipedes, cutworms and leather-jackets to their natural enemies – birds. Destroy any you come across yourself. Many soil pests like wireworms and cutworms can be attracted to traps made from scooped-out potatoes or carrots fixed on skewers just below the soil surface. Examine the traps daily and destroy any pests that have collected there. If a lettuce or other similar plant suddenly keels over, dig it up and you may catch the wireworm or leather-jacket responsible.

Animal pests

Birds Small birds such as sparrows can cause a great deal of damage and can be deterred by planting single strands of strong, black cotton alongside or above seedlings, about 2in (5cm) above the ground. Brightly coloured children's wind-mills are also effective. Larger birds like pigeons are a more serious pest, especially in vegetable and fruit gardens. Wire or plastic netting is the best deterrent – 4–6in (10–15cm) square mesh will keep off pigeons. A net will also keep off cats and dogs, but the drawback is that it stops birds from scavenging for pests. It is therefore better to give temporary protection to vul-nerable crops by placing netting over the wire hoops that are used for low polythene tunnels. (*See also* overleaf for other forms of bird deterrent.) Remember that birds are particularly attracted to young seedlings and newly planted greens such as lettuce, so always put up your protection when sowing or transplanting.

Cats Hawthorn twigs laid on the surface help to protect seedlings from cats as do pea guards.

Mice These mainly attack peas. Traps are the best remedy or you can cover the pea seeds with holly leaves which might deter the mice.

Moles Either place traps in their runs or drive them away by putting moth-balls or pieces of foam rubber soaked in paraffin and set on fire in their runs.

Beneficial Creatures

There are many beneficial creatures that live in the soil or above ground and care must be taken not to destroy these by mis-take. Following is a list of the more com-mon ones and how they help in the garden:

Bees Pollinators.
Carabid beetle Attacks aphids, slugs and snails.
Centipedes Larger and faster than milli-pedes; they eat small slugs, snails and insects.
Common toad Eats slugs and insects.
Devil's coach horse beetle Both the adult and larvae eat soil insects.
Earthworms Generally help aerate and turn the soil to incorporate humus.

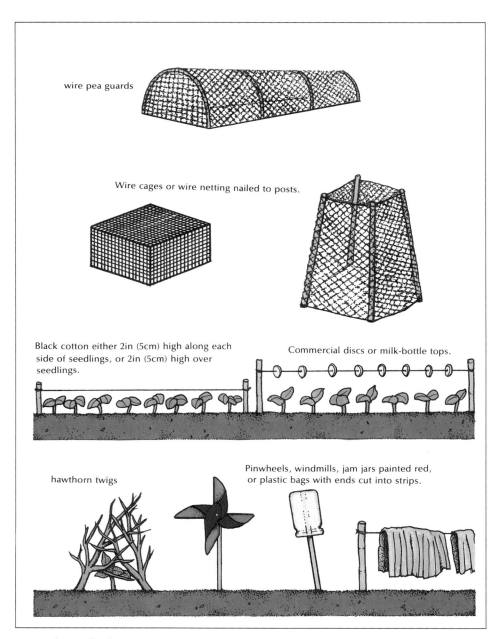

wire pea guards

Wire cages or wire netting nailed to posts.

Black cotton either 2in (5cm) high along each side of seedlings, or 2in (5cm) high over seedlings.

Commercial discs or milk-bottle tops.

hawthorn twigs

Pinwheels, windmills, jam jars painted red, or plastic bags with ends cut into strips.

Various forms of bird scarer.

Garden spider   Eats insects.
Hedgehog   Eats slugs and insects.
Hoverfly   Helps to control aphids.
Hunting spider   Eats many insects.
Ichneumon fly   Lays eggs in moth, beetle and aphid larvae.
Lacewing   Attacks caterpillars and aphids.
Ladybird   Eats aphids.

Parasitic fly   Helps control maybugs.
Parasitic wasp   Controls white caterpillars and aphids.
Predaceous capsid   Feeds on scale insects, aphids and spider mites.
Sail wasp   Lays eggs in the larvae of other insects.

Keep a constant check for pests and diseases to give a healthy vegetable garden.

GLOSSARY

Acid soil A soil which has a pH of below 7.0.

Aeration Free passage of air within the soil.

Alkaline soil A soil which has a pH of above 7.0.

Annual Plant which germinates, grows and sets seed in one season, thus completing its life cycle.

Biennial Plant which grows in the first year, flowers and sets seed in second year.

Catch crop Crop which grows either between maturing plant and one just planted or between a slow-growing and a quick-growing plant.

Chlorosis Yellowing appearance caused by lack of chlorophyll.

Compost a) Well-rotted material used as a soil conditioner which also offers forms of nutrients in small amounts.

b) A mixture of growing mediums such as loam, sand, etc, used for sowing seed (seed compost) or potting on (potting compost).

Cordon Plant (usually fruit tree) trained to grow as a single stem.

Corm A swollen modified stem base, bulb-like in appearance. Shoots grow from bud at top.

Cotyledon First set of leaves produced by seedling. Usually bear no resemblance to final shape of leaf.

Damping down Adding water to surface of bench, pathway, etc, to create a humid atmosphere around aerial section of plant, particularly useful in warm weather.

Deciduous Plant which loses its leaves in dormant season.

Dicotyledon Plant which has two seed leaves.

Dormant The state of being inactive, period when plant growth and manufacturing processes close down.

Espalier Plant (usually fruit tree) which is trained to have a vertical trunk and branches at 12–15½in (30–40cm) intervals.

Evergreen A plant which retains its foliage throughout year.

F₁ hybrid Obtained when two closely-related seed strains are crossed.

Fruiting body Fungus, i.e. mushrooms and bread mould.

Fumigate To disinfect (a glasshouse) using smoke or gas containing a fungicide or an insecticide.

Fungicide A chemical solution used to kill fungus.

Half-hardy Plants which must be protected from frosts.

Hardening off Process by which plants are acclimatized over a period to outdoor or cooler conditions after propagation under glass or in sheltered positions.

Hardy Outdoor plants which will tolerate colder conditions of winter.

Herbaceous A plant which does not form a woody stem.

Humus Brown, glue-like substance derived from the breakdown of vegetation and animal by-products.

Hybrid Two plants from distant species which are crossed to form a new variety.

Inorganic The use of synthetically produced artificial chemicals rather than those derived from natural sources.

Insecticide Chemicals used to control and kill insects.

Internode Distance between one leaf node to the next.

Larva Young of butterflies, moths, etc.

Lateral Side branch which grows from main stem.

Leaching Soluble matter drawn through soil by water and gravity.

Leaf Mould Partially decayed leaves broken down to form a brown, flaky mass.

Monocotyledon Only one seed leaf.

Mulch Layer of straw, leaf mould, etc, around plants which helps retain moisture, keeps weed growth down and protects low-growing fruit such as strawberries.

Naturalizing Plants allowed to grow informally in natural conditions, e.g. daffodils and other bulbs.

Nectar Sweet liquid produced by plants

and in flowers that attract insects, which play a vital role in pollination.

Node Point from which leaves and branches grow.

Organic Natural substances obtained from the breaking down of plant or animal remains.

Pan i) Condition of the soil where heavy watering or rain has caused hard packing of the surface.

ii) Hard layer of soil caused through mechanical cultivation to the same depth each time.

iii) A shallow pot used to grow seedlings.

Parasite Lives off a host plant and is incapable of independent existence.

Peat Substance naturally formed from vegetable remains in wet areas such as bogs.

Perennial Plant which lives indefinitely, such as herbaceous plants.

pH This refers to the percentage of hydrogen ions in the soil; the pH scale enables one to measure acidity levels and determine the type of soil. Neutral stage is 7.0, soil above this point is alkaline, below 7.0 it is acidic. Soil-testing kits can be obtained from garden centres and once soil type is established suitable plants can be chosen accordingly.

Pricking out The planting out of seedlings into larger containers or individual pots. This is only done when they have produced their first set of adult leaves.

Pupa Also known as chrysalid, the stage between larva and adult in butterfly and moth families, etc.

Resting period Dormancy period when plant puts on little or no growth.

Rhizome Underground stem from which roots grow.

Root run Area used by roots of plant.

Rootstock A plant into which a second plant is grafted.

Saprophyte Plant which gains nourishment from decayed organic matter.

Scion Branch or bud which is transferred to a second plant by grafting.

Seedling Young plant.

Self-compatible Plant which does not need pollinating by second plant.

Self-fertile Plant which does not need pollinating by another plant.

Species Type of plant which always grows true to form.

Sphagnum Type of moss which has good water retention facilities.

Spore Tiny reproductive 'cells' of such plants as mosses and ferns, also of some diseases.

Spur Lateral branches which produce sublaterals bearing several flower buds.

Sterile Not producing seeds.

Stopping The removal of the growing tip of a plant to encourage the production of lateral branches.

Strain Plant from a species which is grown by seed.

Stratification Process used to overcome dormancy in seeds of hardy plants which need a cold period before germination. These are planted in a pot in sandy soil and left in a sheltered position or in a coldframe in winter. Stratification can take place during summer by placing seeds in the fridge.

Terminal Usually referring to buds, branches or flowers found at the tip of a stem or branch.

Tilth Crumb-like texture of surface soil, ideally suited to seed sowing.

Top-dressing Addition of fresh soil, or organic fertilizer to the surface of the soil.

Trench Soil dug out up to a depth of 39in (1 metre) for deep-rooting crops.

Under-plant Small plants grown under and around larger ones.

Unisexual Flower containing only female or only male sex organs, not both.

Variegated Leaves which have more than one colour.

Weed Plant which is growing where it is not wanted.

INDEX